PLEASE HELP US TO PROTECT BODMIN MOOR

A few words about walking and access on B There are huge areas of Bodmin
Moor that are unfenced and known as comm ʹ walk
anywhere we wish. The "common" in comm ʹmers
to graze their animals upon these areas – (of
Bodmin Moor is in private ownership, whic⅃ d be
sought before walking across it. We must ke ːmber
that a permissive path is just that – a route fⁱ ʹou to
walk on a temporary basis and which may b ᴉd the
landowner wishes to do so.

CW00735672

Please adhere to the countryside code:

- **Always** take litter home
- **Close** gates after using them
- Stay on the footpaths and use stiles where provided
- **Keep dogs on leads at all times**
- Do not feed livestock
- Guard against all risks of fire
- Help keep water clean

Remember that the farmers on Bodmin Moor have a difficult enough time to make a living
– the farms are generally small, the soils are thin, the rainfall heavy (don't tell everybody!)
and it is they that are responsible for maintaining the wonderful landscape that you are
enjoying. Let's help them keep it so.

If you have enjoyed this book or have discovered something worthy of inclusion in a
reprint, we would be grateful if you could email your comments to bofbmnet@aol.com.

The "Official" Beast of Bodmin Moor

After a good walk it is often nice to sit down with a
cup of tea (or something a little stronger) and a
book with which to relax. May we heartily recom-
mend a book entitled "Written in Jest" by Michael
Lee aka. "The Official Beast of Bodmin Moor".

Michael wrote to the Best of Bodmin Moor asking
for the position of "The Beast" and his book is an
anthology of spoof job applications to various
bodies and their replies. We appointed him to the post in autumn 2002, though his
applications to the Archbishop of Canterbury for the position of Stableboy to the four
horses of the Apocalypse and his application to Tony Blair as "Scapegoat" were less
successful. With a forward by Michael Palin , it is a highly entertaining read, reminiscent
of The Henry Root Letters and it's ISBN no is 1-86105-577-3.

The Best Of Bodmin Moor

SIX WALKS ON AND AROUND BODMIN MOOR

This book contains six walks around the parishes that make up Bodmin Moor. They are all on public rights of way, so do not expect each walk to be over wild open moorland. Although large areas of the moor fall into this description, they are not the best served when it comes to legal rights of way. Instead I have chosen walks that show the rich and varied landscapes, that make up the area classed as Bodmin Moor. There is high moorland if you want it, but there are also wooded valleys and gentle farmland.

The moor contains many archaeological remains and also vast amounts of industrial history. Where possible I have tried to include a scattering of these on each walk. Please remember that many others lie on private land, so although I may mention them they are not always accessible.

Each walk comes with a map, hopefully good enough to guide you round. I have also given brief instructions as to how to reach the start of each walk. However, I would advise purchasing a copy of the OS map for Bodmin Moor (Explorer 109). It really is an invaluable tool if you want to know about the moor, and will help you to discover far more than I can include in this book.

Whatever the weather, make sure you are prepared for the conditions. I researched these walks during December 2002, a particularly wet time on the moor. The proper footwear is essential, with support to the ankles vital. It is just as easy to slip and break something in the summer as it is in the winter. During the summer don't forget to take plenty of water and a hat.

Where possible I have mentioned local shops, post offices and pubs - please make use of them. It is a hard life up on the moor, and often the first thing to go in the community is the village shop (as has recently happened at North Hill). Also if possible why not use public transport to reach the start of the walk. Apart from the St Clether walk all can be reached by bus routes (the Blisland one requires walking from the village). A pilot scheme has been introduced on the west side of the moor called Corlink, this acts like a taxi service, you ring at least an hour ahead of when you need the bus, and it will be there when you arrive. The number for this service is 0845 850 55 66.

Enjoy your walking

Mark Camp

SIX WALKS ON AND AROUND BODMIN MOOR

All walks are graded with stars,
☆ for an easy walk
☆☆☆☆☆ for a strenuous walk.

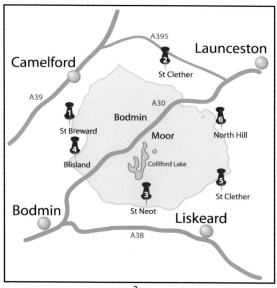

On The Edge
St. Breward

Start of walk	Outside St Breward parish church. Grid Ref SX097774
To get there	The easiest way to reach St Breward is to take the B3266, Bodmin to Camelford road and turn right between St Tudy and Michaelstow. Alternatively turn left off the A30 north of Bodmin. Once you reach St Breward, the church is at the north end of the village. St Breward is served by the Corlink bus service. For details phone 0845 850 5556.
Services	There is a Post office and shop in the village, this also features a local information area.
The Walk	Distance 2½ miles ★★★

The "village" of St Breward stretches out along a ridge running south from the church. It is not so much one village as a collection of hamlets joined together by a road. To the west of the village the terrain drops away to the Camel River, whilst to the east the parish climbs up to the two highest points in Cornwall, Brown Willy and Roughtor. Footpaths and quiet roads lead out onto the open moor but on this walk you will be exploring the ridge where the granite uplands end and the softer, older rocks resume.

The walk starts by heading north; away from the church and past an old AA sign telling you it is 235 miles to London. Nowadays it is an afternoon's drive but when the sign was put up it was a lifetime's adventure!

Soon views open out on all sides; the Camel River can be seen on the left running down past Wadebridge on its way to Padstow and the sea. On a clear day Trevose Head can be seen along with Stepper Point.

Ahead of you the windfarm at Delabole can be seen in the distance, whilst closer, and to the left, sits Michaelstow Beacon with its ruined Iron Age fort on top. To your right the aforementioned Brown Willy and Roughtor can be seen on the far edge of the parish. They are soon lost as the road descends and as it turns a bend to the right, you must go left along a track where a granite boulder bears a memorial inscription. Follow this track until you reach the entrance to a house, here the footpath leads off to the left,

4

down the Camel valley and to the china clay tips on the skyline.

At the bottom of the path a signpost points towards Coombe amongst other places. Following the river (although rarely seen) the path enters woodland through a gate and slowly descends. The sounds of familiar birds are soon replaced by stranger noises and a peek over the wall at the bottom of the hill reveals the source. This is the home of North

following a wall covered in lichen and moss, a good sign of clean air. It is part of the Camelford Way, a waymarked path that runs from Camelford to join the Camel Trail at Wenford Dries. When you reach another marker post (just after an old stile with a very low tree), take the path to the right and head downhill.

This path runs down beside the remains of Great Onslow Consuls Mine. Very little can be seen (there are shafts up by the road) and very little is known of what was a small copper mine in the mid 1800's. As the trees give way to bracken the view opens out

Wood-Sorrel
flowers April to June,
flowers and
leaves close
up at night

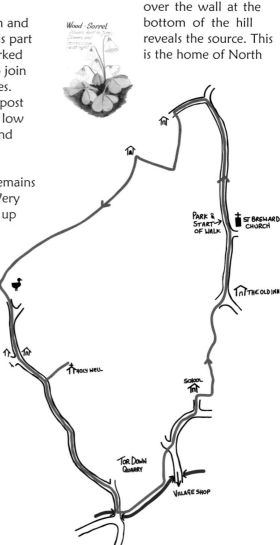

PARK & START OF WALK

ST BREWARD CHURCH

THE OLD INN

HOLY WELL

SCHOOL

TOR DOWN QUARRY

VILLAGE SHOP

5

Cornwall Aviaries and Tropical Bird Farm and a short distance on you will find the entrance. Visitors are welcome when open, not only to see the birds but also guinea pigs, monkeys and llamas.

Past the farm the path winds between the hamlet of Chapel and turns up the hill on the road towards St Breward. After a short distance a footpath goes off to the left. A notice gives

Babbling Brook

Holy Well Entrance

information on the Holy Well and it is worth walking the 75 yrds or so up the hill to view it. After this brief excursion continue up the tarmac road lined by large lumps of granite. After passing some houses even more granite can be seen high on the left. This is the waste

from Tor Down Quarry, the entrance of which is just above the high stone wall further up the road.

Looking in over the gate, the abandoned buildings of the closed down quarry are slowly being engulfed by Buddleia and hide any view of the actual workings. It was from this quarry that stone was taken to build the bleak Bodmin Gaol and at the other extreme the rather grand Naval College at Dartmouth. Signs warning of the dangers of the quarry mark the start of the next footpath to the left of the road. This follows the fast flowing stream which tumbles in natural waterfalls as it cascades over large granite rocks. The quarry is nowhere to be seen and the only danger seems to be from the uneven boulders that line the path as it climbs. It eventually flattens out and turns left above the quarry with the main part of St Breward village stretching out along the ridge behind you. The view towards Wadebridge can again be enjoyed.

Chapel Holy Well

Wild Strawberry

Primrose

Bluebell
flowers April to June

Dog Violet
flowers April to July

St Breward Parish Church

At the end of the path the road is rejoined and the church tower can be seen to the left. Follow the road towards it, shortly turning off down the lane to the school. This fine building is built of Tor Down granite, one of the best examples in the area. Pass it on your left and take the path that winds between the fields to the farm. When you arrive go straight across the yard and out on to the road opposite the Old Inn. This area used to be the market place where sheep and cattle were sold three or four times a year. The Inn itself has been selling beer for 200 yrs and it is said that the village had the name Simonward back in the 1500's, Simon Ward being King Arthur's brewer!

From here it is only a short walk back to the church and the start of the walk,.....but what's the hurry?

Common Hazel

English Oak

Common Holly

The Peaceful Valley
St. Clether

Start of walk	St Clether Church, Grid Ref SX206844
To get there	St Clether can be reached by turning south of the A395 from Launceston to Davidstow, alternatively come off the A30 at Five Lanes and head for Altarnun then onto Laneast and St Clether.
Services	None in the area
The Walk	Distance 1½ miles ★★

The small parish of St Clether lies at the northern edge of the moor, hidden from most travellers. It is a parish of small farmsteads without even a settlement big enough to call a village. At its centre sits the church with only

St Clether Church

the old vicarage to keep it company, and it is here that the walk starts.

The church was rebuilt in the 1800's after a fire almost completely destroyed it in 1865. All that remains from beforehand is the tower, font and pillars. Originally built in the 12th Century, the "modern" church still looks the part as it sits here on the edge of the Inny Valley.

Signs in the churchyard direct you to the Holy Well and chapel, but this walk will take a longer route by following the road up from the church passing the vicarage. This sits facing the church, clad in local slate, as it was when the author Thomas Hardy visited here in the 1870's. He had married Emma Gifford, whose brother in law was the vicar of Boscastle, and who had previously been good friends with a certain William Sergent. The poor William, abandoned by Emma, was now struck down with consumption and was at the time living

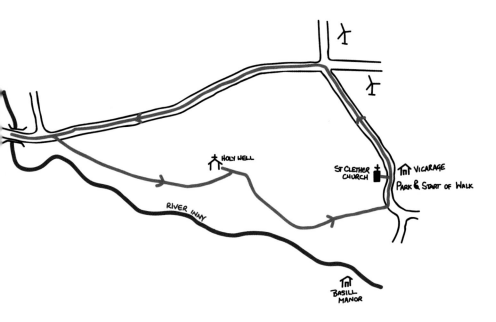

Farming, Old and New

Leaving church and vicarage behind, proceed up the lane. If you turn around you should be able to see the long jagged ridge of Kilmar Tor on the skyline with the TV mast of Caradon Hill behind it. Nearer the top, views to your left include Buttern Hill with Brown Willy just poking out above it whilst to the right of them Roughtor stands proud.

To your right (and ahead) the traditional farming of the moor has been replaced partly by a windfarm. In the past 10 years or so several of these "farms" have been developed in Cornwall, supplying electricity to the local villages and beyond. The Gaia Centre at Delabole is

at the vicarage. It is said that Hardy saw his face peering out of a window and went home and wrote "The Face at the Casement". The fate of William is not known.

9

The Peaceful Valley

to Tregulland. A footpath starts through the gateway on the right and stays on the level as it crosses the field to a stile over the wall. In the next field head straight ahead with the church tower soon coming into view. The path goes below the huge rock outcrop and through a gap in the hedge beside the telegraph pole (be careful of barbed wire). Once through the hedge the chapel can be seen up the hill on your left, make your way up through the bracken to the entrance on the right hand side. Note the watercress growing in the stream that flows from the chapel, a good sign of freshwater.

The St Clether Holy Well and Chapel is the largest of its type in Cornwall. The

worth visiting to find out more about renewable energy.

At the crossroads turn left and follow the lane as it descends between banks criss-crossed with badger runs. These large animals are seldom seen in daylight but an evening stroll in mid-summer may just reward you with a sighting. Badgers or not, this is a lovely quiet lane rich in flora in the spring and summer, and at the bottom it leads to a bridge over the River Inny.

Modern railings belie this bridge's age, but it is worth leaning on them and seeing if you can spot the trout that dart upstream. The Inny runs east across the top of the moor cutting a deep valley on its way to meet the Tamar in woodland below Milton Abbott. Here at St Clether it winds its way downstream between farmed hillsides, with the valley bottom being particularly marshy in winter months.

Primrose
flowers March to May

It is along the valley bottom that the walk now goes, returning from the bridge and past the turning

Brother, can you spare a............?

*Holy Well & Chapel. "This door is like life; never locked
but needs a push to enter"*

site is thought to have originated in the 6th Century when Clederus, one of Brechin of Wales's 24 children came here and set up a hermitage. By the 15th Century the building had fallen into disrepair and was renovated, a process repeated in the late 1800's. The large altar is believed to date from the 15th Century, whilst a plaque resting against the wall dates from 1913 and asks visitors to place 3d in the box for the upkeep of the building. Unless you have a threepenny bit on you, I would suggest leaving a slightly larger donation.

As you leave the site, follow the path through a gate then descend back towards the river. The path takes a large arc around the bracken, then climbs up and under the telegraph line below the church. Across the valley you may just be able to see the roof of Basill Manor, built in the 16th Century and for a long time the home of the Trevelyan family. It is now a residential home for autistic adults with their own farm and craft workshops.

A gate leads out onto the road below the church, be careful if there are sheep about, they are very friendly and will try and follow given half a chance! The house below was once the local school and now belongs to the owners of the sheep who treat them as pets. To finish the walk turn left back up the hill to the church.

Common Polypody
grows on rocks, tree trunks
and on the ground

Hard Fern
grows on acidic soils

11

In Search of White Feathers
St. Neot

Start of walk	St Neot village car park, Grid Ref SX184678
To get there	Leave the A38 at Twowatersfoot and head north up the Loveny valley. The car park can be found at the west end of the village after passing the church and the pub. If coming from the A30, take the Colliford Lake turning just west of Bolventor.
Services	The No 78 bus from Liskeard comes through the village. There is a Post Office/shop and public toilets are in the car park.
The Walk	Distance 3½ Miles ★★★★

Snuggled into its own little valley on the southern edge of the moor, the village of St Neot, like Blisland, hides from the fact that its parish, the 2nd largest in Cornwall, contains vast areas of high moorland. Behind the church, on south facing slopes, a green patchwork of fields stretch off into the distance. Below, the Loveny (or St Neot) River meanders through meadows on its way to join the River Fowey at Twowatersfoot. On the edge of one of these meadows sits St Neot's Holy Well, where the saint is supposed to have caught his daily meal of one fish. He found the area a perfect place to live, and to many it keeps its appeal. In 2002 it was judged the village of the year for south and south-west England.

There are many fine walks in the parish including the Two Valleys Walk, which circles the high ground to the north-east of the village. On the northern edge a footpath runs along the side of Dozmary Pool, said to be bottomless and the setting for the story of King Arthur and his sword Excaliber. To the east lies Golitha Falls, where the Fowey River tumbles down through rich woodland, whilst further upstream Draynes Valley cuts through the centre of the moor.

St Neot Village

12

Restored

The walk in this book follows the Loveny River as it leaves the village, then climbs up to Goonzion Downs before descending back into the village from the south-west. It starts at the village car park where the bus stops and there are also toilets. A road runs below the car park towards Lampen Farm and although the OS map has a footpath marked as leaving the road and crossing a field, it is best to stick to the road. Across the valley there are good views of the church and it should be possible to pick out the oak branch positioned on top of the tower. This tradition signifies the villagers' Royalist support during the Civil War, and every 29th May (Oak Apple Day) the branch is replaced.

Once over a cattle grid the path goes left and runs beside the Loveny River. Past the farm it goes away from the river behind two houses. Both houses have been considerably "improved" over the last few years, the second one being the old mill. The wheel has now been reinstated and a new bridge built over the river, very much in keeping with the surroundings.

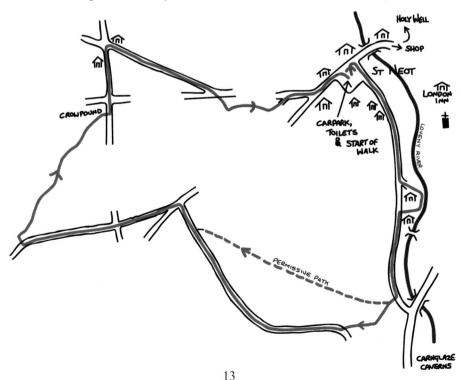

Wheal Mary

Soon the chimney stack of Wheal Mary Mine comes into view. Although mining started here as early as the 1750's, this is all that remains, and dates from the early 1900's when the waste tips of earlier workings were reprocessed. Nowadays St Neot is better known for its slate than its tin, and at the end of the track a short walk down the road leads to Carnglaze, an underground slate quarry that can be visited. During the Second World War the navy stored surplus rum here. Nowadays "The Rum Store" is used to host underground music concerts.

Carnglaze Cavern Entrance   (Circa 1920)

Going back to the walk, a kissing gate on your right, just before you reach the road, gives you two choices. The official footpath goes immediately left and straight up through the trees whilst a permissible path takes an easier route up the valley and through a second kissing gate. This is a conservation walk and may not always be open, please check the signs on the gate.

To follow the official right of way requires a very steep climb up the bank on your left once just inside the gate, The path is not immediately obvious and heads for a wooden stile on the skyline which is not the easiest to negotiate. On reaching the stile (and resting) the path veers slightly to the left as it continues up the hill. Stone steps set into the wall at the top are not easily found but are just to the right of a cut in the wall. With no signpost at present perhaps it is better to just climb over at the easiest place. Once in the next field, head right towards a small stone barn. The footpath gains the road via a gateway hidden behind the curve of a wall on your left. Now turn right.

Heading away from Polmenna Farm, the road reaches an ancient gateway and then a modern cattle grid. Here the permissive path, from down in the valley, rejoins the walk, and at the road junction take the second left. This leads to a crossroads high on Goonzion Downs.

Goonzion is believed to mean dry place downs in Cornish, so the addition of downs to the name is unnecessary. Walking up here in early January it is hard to see how it got its name! Go straight across at the crossroads and descend towards the house called Luna (you should be able to see the roof over the trees). This is believed to be the site of the original Doomsday manor of Fawitona. On the skyline the clay tips above St Austell stand prominent, whilst to the right the village of Mount and further on the Churchtown of Warlegan can be seen.

When another cattle grid is reached, turn right and follow the fence to a gate where a footpath leads uphill over the downs. It is easy enough to follow as it climbs between overgrown piles of mine waste and fenced off shafts. It is said that St Neot told his fellow villagers that whoever found minerals up here would become so rich they would be able to shoe their horse in silver. After many failed attempts St Neot said he would place a white feather on the spot where the mineral lode lay. The following morning the downs were covered in white feathers and that's why there are holes all over the area! Do not venture away from the path. Although most of the mining was only done in shallow pits there were some shafts sunk up here by Wheal Friendship in the mid 1800's and care should be taken.

The road is reclaimed again via a gate, and after passing through it, turn left. This leads to a crossroads at Crowpound. The name comes from the overgrown remains to the left of the road, probably a medieval cattle enclosure, but legend has it that St Neot sent the crows of the parish here during sermons so that the local farmers had no excuse to abstain. Just west of here is a larger settlement called the "Roman Camp", it has now mostly disappeared under the plough and is thought to be earlier in date than Roman, possibly Iron Age. A better preserved Iron Age settlement can be visited to the north of the village on Berry Down.

Leaving Crowpound and its standing stone behind you, go straight ahead (signposted Colliford Lake) until you reach the next junction. Here turn right and follow the road downhill with good views of the village dominated by the church. When you reach yet another cattle grid cross the road and take the path that follows the post and rail fence (on your left) before turning left through a small gate, it then winds left of the field between a wall and large rhododendron bushes. Cross the next field keeping to the left and then over a wooden stile and down some stone steps onto a drive. From here you rejoin the road and descend into the village and the car park where the walk started.

Standing Stone Next to Crowpound

Two Bridges Walk
Blisland

Start of walk	North Kerrow, Blisland, Grid Ref SX114748
To get there	From the A30 turn off opposite the Temple turning, this takes you out across Manor Common. Follow the road past the turning to Hawks Tor Farm and the turning to Bradford. The next left goes to Blisland, ignore it and park on the side of the road anywhere along the next stretch. If coming from Blisland, North Kerrow is north-east of the village and can be reached by a selection of roads.
Services	A Post Office can be found in Blisland village. Corlink bus service serves the village and can be contacted on 0845 8505556.
The Walk	Distance 2½ Miles ✫

With its village green surrounded by church and inn, Blisland has often been said to be more English than Cornish. Sitting outside the pub on a summer's afternoon one could easily forget that the wild expanse of the moor is only a mile or so away. The view from the green is of a wooded valley, giving a pleasant backdrop to the church, but much of the parish is made up of open moorland, home to the hardy few

BLISLAND
TO COMMEMORATE THE
MILLENNIUM 2000
AND TO CELEBRATE
THE GOLDEN JUBILEE
OF HER MAJESTY
THE QUEEN
6th FEBRUARY 2002

and far from the English idyll.

The walk starts at Kerrow, just one of the many settlements that litter this area of the moor. Surrounded by a small group of fields, which have been poached from the open moorland, at one time each house would have had enough land to be self-sufficient. Nowadays all of the land probably belongs to one farm and the fields used for nothing more than grazing. Head east from Kerrow, out onto the open moor with views over towards Brown Willy. With no hedges it is easy to think that walkers

Granite and....................

..........Gorse feature heavily on this walk

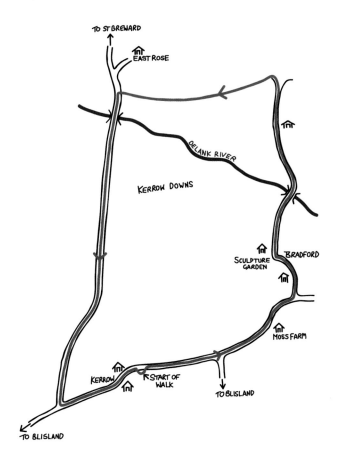

have a right to walk anywhere, but all this land belongs to someone and it is only the Commoners who can legally leave the road and cross the moor. Commoners' rights go back to medieval times when the lord of the manor was required to set aside some land where the peasants could gather food and fuel. Nowadays the only right that the Commoners still seem to exercise is that of pasture, and chances are you will have seen sheep, cattle or horses roaming the open moor. Other rights include turbury, the cutting of turf (or peat), piscary, to take fish from lakes and streams, and estovers, the right to take cuttings of wood and bracken.

So with legal access to the open moor only permissive, you must follow the road down towards Moss Farm. As you do, look onto the skyline ahead of you. Carbilly Tor, with its disused quarry sits centre, but to the right of it you should be able to make out the Trippet Stones. These stand on the horizon looking like a group of men and are all that remain of a stone circle that once comprised 26 stones.

17

Carbilly Quarry

This is the DeLank River, fed by the waters of Roughtor Marsh; it runs under the old clapper bridge here and onward towards the River Camel below St Breward. The fact that the bridge is here at such a quiet spot shows that it hasn't always been this quiet. This was once an important route, running up the DeLank Valley linking all the little

Bradford Bridge

As the lane drops down to Moss Farm, you can see how perhaps the farm got its name. The sunken banks of the lane are covered in a verdant layer of mosses and lichen, even in mid-winter. Past the farm, take the left turn by the phone box. This leads down to Bradford and the unusual Wilderness Sculpture Garden that can be visited most times of the year. Bradford is said by EC Axford in his book "Bodmin Moor", to be "one of the loveliest places on the moor", and with the sun shining through the trees and the stream playing over the granite he might be right.

settlements along the way. Nowadays the road only runs to just up behind the bungalow, where it turns into a private track before petering out in a field. Most of the settlements that it would have served have disappeared, now only a name on the map or a ragged collection of low walls.

Pulling yourself away from the river, cross the bridge and head up the lane

Looking towards Brown Willy and Rough Tor

Delphi Bridge

past the bungalow. At the top, the track carries on through a gate marked private, but to the left another gate, (also marked private) has a stile tucked away beside it. Finally you can leave tarmac behind and follow a footpath as it crosses the top of four fields, stiles connecting each one. Over the hill ahead of you are the DeLank quarries, the only ones still working in the area (you may also be able to hear them). Granite from these quarries was used in the construction of lighthouses at Beachy Head, Bishop's Rock and out on the Eddystone.

Once over the last stile, cross what can be a wet area in the winter, to the road. This is a quiet, yet popular road into St Breward, and do be aware of traffic. The farm to your right is East Rose and from March to November the owners serve light meals, cream teas and ice cream between 9am and dusk. If you can ignore the temptation, head left to Delphi Bridge (named Delford on OS maps). A sister bridge to Bradford, this is another fine place to sit and let time fly by.

The route back to the start continues up the hill, with Kerrow Downs on the left. A path seems to run alongside the road

amongst the gorse bushes, an escape from the traffic. Hidden amongst the gorse are the remains of old settlements, field systems and even tumuli (burial sites), none of which I could see from the road.

When you reach a T-junction, turn left. This will lead you back to Kerrow, the road winding up between the old enclosed fields. With the walk finished it is worth going into Blisland village to view the church and perhaps visit the pub, which has had many accolades festooned on it in recent years, not least National Pub of the Year.

The Blisland Inn

Quoits, Crows and Copper
St Cleer

Start of walk	Crows Nest Inn, Crows Nest. Grid Ref SX264 694
To get there	By road, either turn left off the B3254 at Fore Down or if coming from the west turn right off the Dobwalls/Minions road, a little after the Common Moor turning. There is usually space to park on the road opposite the inn car park
Services	Occasional bus services from Liskeard run through the village, stopping outside the inn. There is a Post Office and shop in Darite.
The Walk	Distance 3½ Miles ✭✭✭

This walk takes place in St Cleer parish, which saw great changes in the 19th century with the discovery of copper on Caradon Hill. It lies on the southern edge of the moor, a mixture of rugged moorland and enclosed farmland. The walk mirrors these features in a smaller scale, taking the walker along winding lanes through farmland, before climbing to overlook what was the richest copper mine in east Cornwall. Along the way you will also see possibly the oldest man-made construction in Cornwall, Trethevy Quoit.

The walk starts outside the Crows Nest Inn and heads off east along the road towards Tokenbury Corner. This road is a dividing line between the enclosed fields on your right and Caradon Hill on your left. On a clear day the views across the farmlands of south-east Cornwall are quite extensive.

You will get a better view once you turn right down the track to Higher Trethake Farm and once past the farm the track broadens out into a lovely green lane. To the south-east you may be able to pick out Rame Head, guarding the entrance to Plymouth Sound from westerly winds, whilst over to your right you can see the tower of St Cleer church. The lane proceeds down between the fields to Lower Trethake Farm where you turn left

Medieval Window

along a road. Lower Trethake is the older of the two farms, there once being a medieval manor here, and a window from the original building is built into the low barn that runs beside the road.

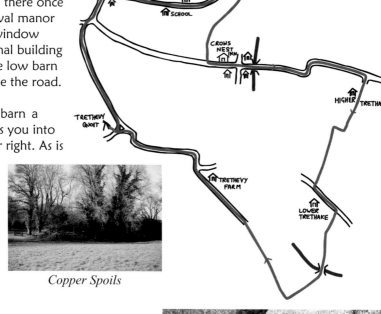

Just after the barn a signpost directs you into a field on your right. As is common with many farms, you pass a selection of rusting implements and assorted odds and ends. At the bottom of the field another

Copper Spoils

low barn stands on its own. Pass to the right of it and through a gate.

You now enter a field, which has a large mound in its centre. This is thought to be a waste tip for the Caradon Copper Mine, a little known mine that was active in the 1850's. The wall on your left runs into what appears to be the bottom of a chimney stack though there are no other signs of mine buildings in the area. The path carries on down to the bottom of the field where it goes over a stile beside the gate. A small stream flows down on your right side until you are able to cross it on a stone "bridge". Now climb to a stile and then descend to the Seaton River. This is a lovely spot to sit and take in the surroundings and it is also the lowest point of the walk. Once

Resting Place

you cross the wonderful old stone bridge, it is a steady climb up the side of the field to a wall stile at the top. This is found on your right just before the gate. Climb over it and head across the field to the opposite side where a similar stile takes you into another field. This smaller field is crossed into the

bottom corner where yet another wall stile leads onto a muddy lane.

The lane is followed to Trethevy Farm, but keep an eye out on the right hand side for views of Trenouth where a mill used to harness the waters of the Seaton River for grinding corn. When you reach Trethevy Farm it won't take you long to realise it is still very much a working farm. You will be lucky to get through with clean shoes! The right of way goes straight on, to the left of the farmhouse, through three gates. Please make sure you close any gates you go through.

When you reach the road turn left and climb gently up to Trethevy Quoit. This ancient burial site can be found in the

Trethevy Quoit

field opposite the road you have just walked up. It is hard to miss! It dates from around 4000 BC and would have been a burial chamber for possibly a whole family, not just one person. Originally it would have been covered in earth, but this disappeared many years ago, as has any trace of its occupants. Many would associate this with the Hurlers Stone Circles up on the moor at Minions, but they were probably erected 2000 years afterwards, the equivalent of the birth of Christ to the present day!

Leaving the stones, turn left up the road towards Darite. This village grew up like many others in the area because of the mining, and if we cross the road and walk up towards the houses facing us, look over the walls on your right. These are the gardens of the miners' cottages where they would have grown all their food. No popping into Liskeard to the supermarket when they needed something for tea. At the bottom of the garden ran a railway line that eventually ended on the quay at Looe and these cottages go under the name of Railway Terrace.

To continue the walk, turn right behind the cottages and follow the road upwards passing the modern school, the village shop and post office. The old cottages give way to modern bungalows with built-on conservatories as you reach the top of the road. After a left-hand bend a sign directs the walker down a bridleway to the right. Stop here and look out across the area in front of you. These are the remains of South Caradon Mine where copper was found in 1836 and it soon became

South Caradon Mine

the richest mine in the area. Today the engine houses that once contained some of the finest engineering Cornwall could produce stand lonely and in danger of falling down. The shafts that men descended to reach the rich ores are clogged up with rusting metal and builders' waste and the dressing floors where the ore was laid out, prior to being shipped down to Looe by rail, have disappeared under a layer of gorse. All is quiet now where once stamping mills would have battered the rock into fine dust. This is what made the villages around here. In the years between 1830 and 1860 the population of St Cleer parish went from around 900 to 3900, at a time when the average life expectancy was only 22 years!

Leaving the ghosts in peace, take the path down towards Crows Nest. Twice it crosses the old railway lines, now incorporated into local gardens in many places. A plan to create a trail along the old route had to be cancelled because of this "poaching" of land over the years. At the bottom of the path turn left along the road and soon you will be back at the Crows Nest Inn, and time for some refreshments.

In the Hawk's Shadow
North Hill

Start of walk	North Hill Church, main gate, Grid Ref SX273766
To get there	North Hill lies just off the B3254, Liskeard to Launceston road. There is limited room to park beside the Church, but there is also a car park a little further on beyond it.
Services	DAC coaches run a regular bus service through the village. Phone 01822 834571 to check for times.
The Walk	Distance 4 Miles ✮✮✮✮✮

As you will gather by reading and using this book, public rights of way out onto the high moor are few and far between. When a path does stray from the enclosed farmlands it tends to come to an abrupt stop in the middle of nowhere. This is no good if you want a circular walk. This walk, from North Hill, does give you a chance to discover the rough magic of the moor, and never use the same path twice. It is quite a strenuous walk, and also goes over some very rough terrain so walking boots are essential.

Old Methodist Chapel

The walk starts in the village of North Hill, a village that you can explore at the end of the walk. From the Church gate head south past what used to be the village Post Office and down the road past the Methodist Chapel. A date on the wall tells us that the building was built in 1810, when Wesley's influence was strong in the area. It is now a private house. Just below the chapel a footpath leaves the road on the right hand side. It winds between two houses before reaching a field where views open out across the Lynher valley and up onto the moors.

The path descends the field to a stile into the woods, just left of the tall trees. You will soon hear the sound of the

Wobbly Bridge

river as you cross a track and head for a bridge. There are in fact two bridges here. The first crosses a millstream whilst the second crosses the main river. It is a narrow bridge and wobbles as you cross it, but I think it's safe!

The River Lynher is fed by streams that come off East Moor to the north west of this walk. It flows along the eastern edge of Bodmin Moor before cutting through East Cornwall, passing St Germans and entering the Tamar below Saltash. Here in the valley below North Hill, it is a wide but reasonably shallow river, still in it's early stages. Leaving the river, the path climbs through the wood before some steps lead you into a field. Keep to your right as you climb up to a stile then cross a farm track that leads to East Castick. Over another stile and up through more woods, you will eventually, after a long climb, emerge onto a tarmaced road.

This road must be one of the most undulating in Cornwall as the humps in it bear scratch marks where vehicles have bottomed out as their unsuspecting owners attempted to drive up onto the moor. At a gentler pace,

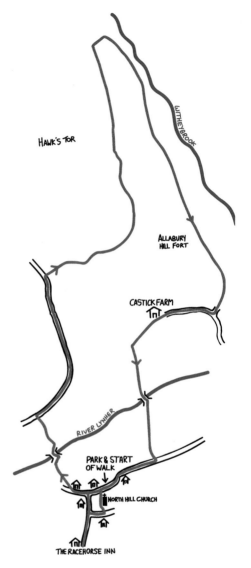

you turn right and climb up the road for about ½ a mile. Here a footpath on your right takes you through a gate and off across an area of rough ground. This can get muddy in the winter but a recent layer of hardcore has improved things for a short distance. Follow the path, passing a small hut after about 100 yards. Very soon you will enter a field. Notice the "wall" in the centre and the mounds of rock. Keep to the top side and when you enter the second half of the field you will see a small gate ahead of you.

Going through this gate you will soon realise why there were so many stones piled up in the fields. The ground is covered in them and any attempt at clearing the area for farming would have necessitated lots of hard work. This rough track now follows the contour of the hillside as it works its way round below Hawk's Tor. The hillside here is covered in the thick vegetation of Rhododendron bushes, nowadays regarded as something of a problem here in the West Country. As you make your way through the "forest" the path descends over large slabs and then, below the summit rocks, it veers to the right. Do not follow it at this point; instead go onwards through the rough ground. It is not easy to

Napoleonic Stone Wall

follow the footpath, but if you keep heading for the lower side of Trewortha Tor you should eventually arrive at a gap in a wire fence. Go through this. Keeping to the same direction head forward until you come to a stone wall. The footpath turns right and follows the wall down to the Withybrook. The terrain is rough and marshy and best avoided by cutting back down the valley before you reach

Hawk's Tor

River Lynher

To the right, and above the track is Allabury, an Iron Age round (or encampment). It is a large circular bank with a ditch on its outer side, with some fine old oak trees growing around the top. It is thought that it was used to keep animals in, as well as their owners, who would come up here in the warmer months to graze on the moor. The "round" is on private land so please do not go exploring.

the bottom of the field. You must head back the way you came, only lower down the field. The wire fence, which you passed through, connects to a stone wall and there is an old wooden stile to climb over. Just to the left of the stile is a stone enclosure built onto the wall but who knows what it was used for and how long ago is was built?

This field brings easy walking and you should head towards the top side of the woods in the distance. Note the wall that appears in the centre of the field and then quickly disappears. It has a purpose and when you get close take a good look, you will see that it hides a pipeline. This was built in the 1930s and carries water all the way to Liskeard. The pipe, hidden from view, will now take the same route as you as it descends into the valley. To do this, continue towards the top edge of the field and pass through a gate before descending to another gate at the edge of the wood. Here the path follows the woodland edge, eventually entering an enclosed area. All these large stone walls that surround the woodland are thought to be the work of Napoleonic prisoners of war.

The enclosed path leads down to a metal gate; here it narrows and then passes through an area of large boulders and oak saplings. Below you, to the left, you may catch glimpses of the Withybrook as it hurtles over rocks on its way down to meet the Lynher. The woods around here are a mixture of trees, and belong to the Trebartha Estate. The estate was bought in the 1940's by the Latham family who continue to run it as a forestry business. A sign informs you of private forestry land when you reach a crossroads of paths. You must take the lowest path, which bends right, to a gate.

A concrete road climbs to Castick Farm, very much a typical moorland farm. It is owned by the Trebartha Estate but is run by a tenant. Keeping the main barns and the farmhouse to your right, proceed through the yards, bearing slightly right and after crossing an open space full of obsolete farm machinery climb a

On a Clear Day.........

more. It was pulled down in the early 1950s after it had been used to accommodate Second World War refugees from Italy. The story goes that they did so much damage that it was cheaper to take down than restore.

Our route goes right and back to North Hill, and eventually to the church. Although the church is not often open it is worth walking through the churchyard and round to the old part of the village on the far side. Leaving by some steps, turn right, then left and walk down the road past some interesting buildings to the Racehorse Inn. Here you can refresh yourselves before heading back to the start of your walk.

stile and descend a wooden ladder. This brings you into a field which you cross to the bottom left hand corner. Head towards the bottom corner of the wood in the next field, go through a gate and turn left and follow the hedge down.

Looking ahead you should be able to see the church at North Hill on the skyline. The Lynher lies below you, and after going through another gate proceed straight across the next field to a bridge over the river.

As you leave the bridge veer slightly right as you walk past the tree in the middle of the field. The footpath ascends through the woods from beside the wall at the top edge of the field; it is not that easy to spot from the bridge but easy enough to find once you gain the wall.

Through the trees it leads to a stile which you cross and then head straight ahead to the road. This is the road from North Hill to the hamlet of Trebartha, built to provide housing for the estate workers. The buildings are all built in the same style but sadly the main house is no

North Hill Church